Sorting
and Sets

by Henry Pluckrose

Gareth Stevens Publishing
A WORLD ALMANAC EDUCATION GROUP COMPANY

Please visit our web site at: www.garethstevens.com
For a free color catalog describing Gareth Stevens' list of high-quality books
and multimedia programs, call 1-800-542-2595 (USA) or 1-800-461-9120 (Canada).
Gareth Stevens Publishing's Fax: (414) 332-3567.

Library of Congress Cataloging-in-Publication Data

Pluckrose, Henry Arthur.
    Sorting and sets / by Henry Pluckrose. — North American ed.
      p. cm. — (Let's explore)
    Includes bibliographical references and index.
    ISBN 0-8368-2966-2 (lib. bdg.)
    1. Set theory—Juvenile literature. [1. Set theory.] I. Title.
  QA248.P583   2001
  511.3'22—dc21   2001031119

This North American edition first published in 2001 by
Gareth Stevens Publishing
A World Almanac Education Group Company
330 West Olive Street, Suite 100
Milwaukee, WI 53212 USA

This U.S. edition © 2001 by Gareth Stevens, Inc. Original edition © 1999 by Franklin Watts.
First published in 1999 by Franklin Watts, 96 Leonard Street, London, EC2A 4XD, United
Kingdom. Additional end matter © 2001 by Gareth Stevens, Inc.

Series editor: Louise John
Series designer: Jason Anscomb
Series consultant: Peter Patilla
Gareth Stevens editor: Monica Rausch
Gareth Stevens designer: Katherine A. Kroll

Picture credits: Steve Shott Photography cover and title page, pp. 4, 5, 7, 9, 17, 19, 20, 23,
24, 25, 27, 29; Bubbles p. 12 (Ian West); Image Bank pp. 11 (Michael Melford), 31 (Jody
Dole); Tracy Morgan Animal Photography p. 15.

With thanks to our models: Reid Burns, Karim Chehab, Alex Dymock, Danielle Grimmett-
Gardiner, Tom Grylls, Hattie Hundertmark, Charlie Newton, and Laura Wynn.

Printed in the United States of America

1 2 3 4 5 6 7 8 9 05 04 03 02 01

Contents

4

We can group, or sort, objects in many different ways. We can sort them by color or by size or by shape. We can even sort objects by how we use them.

When we sort objects, we make sets. A set is a group of objects that are the same, or similar, in some way. What is the same about these objects?

When we sort objects, we can look for features that are alike. We can also look for features that are different. How are these boats alike? How are they different?

9

Sometimes we use sets to make objects easier to find. These fruits and vegetables are sorted into sets. Can you find the strawberries? Can you find the green beans?

In a library, books are sorted into groups. Books about similar subjects are placed close to each other on the shelves so the books will be easier to find.

If we sort these dogs by size, we can make two sets — one set of adults and one set of puppies. Can you sort these dogs another way?

15

Sometimes we sort objects by the patterns they have. Can you help Kate find the sock that matches the one she is wearing?

17

We can sort objects by shape. Look at this plate of cookies. How many different sets of shapes can you find? In what other ways can you sort these cookies?

We often can sort a large set of objects into smaller sets. This set is a group of toys. Can you sort the toys into smaller sets?

23

This jar is full of buttons. Most of these buttons can belong to more than one set.

You can sort the buttons
by color . . .

or by shape.

What other way can you sort them?

All the pieces of candy in the red circle are pink. All the pieces of candy in the blue circle have wrappers. The pieces that are in both circles are pink and have wrappers. These pieces of candy belong to both sets.

Look at this bouquet of pretty flowers. The flowers are many different colors, sizes, and types. How can you sort these flowers into sets?

29

What color is each butterfly? Are the butterflies all the same size? Are they all the same shape? These questions help us find out what type each butterfly is. Sorting tells us more about our world.

Index

More Books to Read

A First Book about Mixing and Matching. Look and Learn (series). Nicola Tuxworth (Gareth Stevens)
Seaweed Soup: Matching Sets. MathStart (series). Stuart J. Murphy (HarperCollins Juvenile)
Sorting. Mortimer's Math (series). Karen Bryant-Mole (Gareth Stevens)